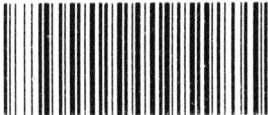

CW01431808

Afterthoughts

by the same author

THE UNFINISHED HARAULD HUGHES
HARAULD HUGHES: THE MODELS TRILOGY
HARAULD HUGHES: FOUR FILMS
HARAULD HUGHES: PLAYS, PROSE, PIECES, POETRY
AYOADE ON TOP
THE GRIP OF FILM
AYOADE ON AYOADE
THE DOUBLE (WITH AVI KORINE)

Richard Ayoade

Afterthoughts

or

Some Pistachios Won't Open

Wisdom for
the Unreflective

faber

First published in 2025
by Faber & Faber Ltd
The Bindery, 51 Hatton Garden
London EC1N 8HN
Published in the USA in 2025

Typeset by Faber & Faber Ltd
Printed and bound by CPI Group (UK) Ltd, Croydon, CR0 4YY

A CIP record for this book
is available from the British Library

ISBN 978–0–571–39820–1

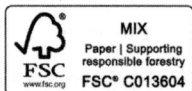

2 4 6 8 10 9 7 5 3

Contents

To Begin:
A Colloquy for One

In search of wisdom, I turn inwards. And yet I cannot find myself. So, I search. I look within.

Are you hoping to find wisdom inside yourself?

Yes.

Is it wisdom that you once had but have since lost, or is it a new kind of wisdom that you're hoping to discover?

If I knew the answer, I wouldn't need to search.

Are you sure the wisdom is inside you?

Yes.

How do you 'do' this searching?

I write.

You write?

Yes.

What do you write about?

I write about the search.

How's that different to just searching?

Shhh.

Okay, but that doesn't really answer the—

Why deny humanity the chance to better itself?

Must I have a reason?

Will you help me in my search? My search for me? For my unique and liberating truth?

To be honest, I think my role is just to give you feed lines.

You're right. Will you accept my search as a gift?

Do I have a choice?

Do I?

Is there anything else you would like to say before you begin sharing these important words?

Yes: I have a caveat.

What is this crucial qualification? Speak, sage.

Although (perhaps) these humble jottings may not have the cultural impact of certain biblical narratives, I cannot prevent scholars from drawing parallels. Nor can I stop people using this volume as a manual for living, or as the basis of a new religion. All I can do is present these words in all humility and let history decide how best to honour me.

Thank you.

Thank you. For joining me on the search.

In what way have I—

Shhh . . .

Part One

Ways of Being:
A Quick Set-Up Guide

THREE FIRST THINKS

1. What is thought? Something to bear in mind.

2. Where do thoughts come from? And what should we do with them?

They come at night. When we're on our trampolines. We must catch them, lest they fall into the cracks of our misremembrances. Those cracks are deep and hard to access with conventional suction nozzles.

3. A thought is as real as a bullet, and even harder to remove from your head.

THINKING ONLINE

1. Where's the box to tick if you *are* a robot?

2. Now, when 'chatting to an expert online', you can ask to 'talk to a human'. But, in conversation, the same request can be taken badly.

THE CASE FOR HAPPINESS

1. Happiness is the only thing that multiplies when you share it. That and venereal disease.

2. Be so happy that, when other people look at you, they become happy too. But not so happy that they become jealous. What you're looking for is a kind of stupid happy that no one envies.

3. Things in themselves don't make us happy, but we can use them to make others unhappy, so they're worth hanging on to.

4. Happiness is the shopfront of self-righteousness.

DOES IT PAY TO THINK ABOUT MONEY?

1. If money talks, what is it saying?

2. If money talks and wealth whispers, poverty must shut up.

3. Life is like a river – sooner or later, it all drains into the bank.

4. They say life is a loan, but a loan has interest.

5. All that glitters is not gold, e.g. glitter.

6. A good example of something that glitters that isn't gold is a turd with glitter in it.

7. Money isn't everything. But everything can be exchanged for money.

8. Old money is like a stagnant pond. There's always something rotten hidden out of sight.

9. It's important to give back, but not so much that we lose our position of dominance.

10. By the time you can afford it, you're too old to enjoy it.

11. By the time you can afford it, you should be old enough to know you don't need it.

12. By the time you can afford it, you should be wise enough to know you shouldn't buy it.

13. Bankruptcy is to businessmen as adult baptism is to evangelicals.

THREE BIG QUESTIONS YOU SHOULD BE ASKING YOURSELF MORE OFTEN

1. Is it okay to forgive the questionable statements of the untalented?

2. When you ask a cabin crew attendant if you can use the lavatory before take-off, and he tells you to be quick, what adjustment is he hoping you'll make?

3. If preparation is all, how can it still be preparation?

THREE SHORTER (BUT STILL BIG) QUESTIONS

1. Which foot is the front one?

2. If you can search the internet, why can't you hide on it?

3. Without the foam, was that really a party?

LIFE: VARIOUS APPROACHES

1. In life you're born in the middle of the race, before you can walk, and you have no shoes, and you can't control your bowels, and also everyone is booing, and maybe you're in the wrong race.

2. Life is a case of mistaken identity.

3. The ideal life is the one we're not living.

4. If life is an illusion, it's a lousy trick.

5. If life keeps giving you lemons, maybe it's not an accident. Maybe you're a grocer, and that's not life; that's your wholesaler.

6. Imagine what life would be like if God hated us.

7. In total, the best years of our lives barely add up to a month.

8. Those who say that life's too short haven't lived very long.

IS OUR PERCEPTION LIMITED?

1. If free will is an illusion, why are you still pressing charges?

2. Beauty, they say, is in the eye of the beholder. But I sometimes wonder: what else is in that eye? I bet there's at least some gunk.

3. If you keep facing the sun, you can't see a shadow. Or anything, really.

THE SOCIAL CONTRACT

1. It's such a privilege to live in this country, but it's not the kind of privilege that feels good to share.

2. One day, inequality will be eradicated, but, until then, we should just try to enjoy it.

3. The old often worry about the way the world is going, perhaps because they are running out of time to ruin it in person.

4. There's something pessimistic about progressivism. To say things can keep getting better might be to imply nothing is ever good enough.

5. A civilisation relies – relies absolutely – on the coherence of the lies it tells itself.

FIVE THINGS WE'VE LEARNED
FROM OUR BODIES

1. 'Better late than never' does not apply w/r/t infections.

2. The roof of the mouth doesn't keep it from getting wet.

3. The skin is the largest organ in the body, and – more's the pity – most cannibals just throw it away.

4. Cold hands can also mean a stopped heart.

5. If the body keeps the score, the best you can hope for is a draw.

FUN: TWO THOUGHTS

1. Fun is, first and foremost, a noun.

2. Fun is joy's trivial brother.

SHOULD WE WORRY ABOUT DEATH BEFORE THE EVENT?

1. Death is not something we should fear; it's life we should be afraid of.

2. If you don't die 'too young', it means everyone was just *waiting*.

3. The worst thing about death is the long hours.

4. To be alive is to know how close one is to death. Wait, that's dying. Maybe I don't know what being alive is like.

IN PRAISE OF HATRED

1. You can't live on spite. But it's a good way of giving life a focus.

2. You've got to be cruel to be kind. And you have to be cruel to be cruel. The important thing to stress is that if you get cruelty right, everything flows from that.

3. Say what you like about hate, it's certainly durable.

TIME: AN ANALYSIS

1. Time is a great teacher, but She's always too late.

2. We are all products of our time, and we spend most of our time making products that will soon be out of date.

3. Time may be a great healer, but She's a terrible dentist.

4. It still takes time to make something timeless.

EIGHTY-EIGHT MOSTLY MISCELLANEOUS MATTERS

1. Everything in moderation still sounds like a lot.

2. A pessimist is an optimist in disguise – a disguise that will never work.

3. If Socrates came back from the dead and opened a fast-food restaurant, a good name for it would be Maxim Chicken.

4. They say pride comes before a fall, as does, it's worth mentioning, wet decking.

5. Bone idleness is inactivity at its most effective.

6. Through the colander of piety drips the curdled juice of self-regard.

7. The phrase 'love is blind' did not originate in the blind community.

8. Just remember: 'The pen is mightier than the sword' is just something someone wrote. Probably some nerd whom you could crush like a cheese puff.

9. One thing we've learned from statues is that the first thing to go is the arms.

10. Once you've had a surprise, what's it called? A disappointment.

11. The thing about not getting dressed is that, after a while, it starts to feel like a victory.

12. They say that no matter how much you try to hold on to something, one day it will be all gone. Apart from resentment. That you get to keep.

13. The same people who say winners don't give up on their dreams call you a loser for sleeping all day.

14. Anger is a great way of getting over the shame of gratitude.

15. Everything has its season, especially seasons.

16. We must find our own purpose, before someone else's purpose finds us.

17. We are more desiring than desirable.

18. Nothing's so good that it's not better when it ends.

19. In fact, to start something is to wish it will end.

20. To be thought truly wise is rare, but it's amazing how much slack people will cut you if you're rich.

21. A complaint is an act of hope that someone will care enough to shut you up.

22. If the joke's not on you, it's on you.

23. All is vanity, except for the noble art of generalisation.

24. If someone can do no wrong, they're not anyone.

25. The use of the word 'performative' tends to be performative.

26. They used to say that a stranger is just a friend you haven't met. And then they met some of those strangers.

27. The milk of human kindness is not safe to drink.

28. Dry cleaning is the closest we have to the Wild West.

29. Don't confuse going deeper with going inwards.

30. Depths don't catch the light.

31. We must actively defend our right to disengage.

32. The 'outrageous' occupy the exhausting intersection between extroversion and self-regard.

33. If the biggest obstacle you face is in your head, you may need surgery.

34. We call the ideas we don't like 'ideologies'.

35. History is what happens to dead people.

36. The difference between being spiritual and being religious is that no one says they're religious.

37. Those who worry about something not being a 'good look' do not seem overly concerned about something being good.

38. Process, not product, partic. w/r/t processed products.

39. Medical check-ups should be called 'pre-mortems'.

40. If someone says, 'Never say never,' it's worth pointing out that they just did.

41. The word 'mostly' emphasises the exception.

42. We do not choose our concerns, but we can choose to ignore the concerns of others.

43. A bird in the hand is bad news for your hand.

44. The best cure for admiration is to encounter its object.

45. The saying 'All things must pass' will not get you through security.

46. Discretion is the shopfront of deception.

47. Ironically, the debate about 'woke' is very tiring.

48. An Englishman's castle is rarely his home, if only for tax purposes.

49. You could say failure makes you resilient, or you could get a different surgeon.

50. They say there's truth in wine, but that's not true.

51. They say there's truth in wine, but those people are drunk.

52. They say there's truth in wine. And also lies. A lot of fall-down, scream-your-head-off lies.

53. Holidays are for people who don't want to be anywhere in particular.

54. When you forgive, you can forget. But if you forget first, there's no need to forgive.

55. Perhaps you're entitled to your opinions; or perhaps you're entitled and opinionated.

56. Those who see everyone as a type don't see anyone in particular.

57. Whitewashing is the closest secular people come to baptism.

58. If everyone likes you, it's probably not you they like.

59. Whoever said 'Cheats never prosper' is cheating themselves out of a comprehensible relationship with reality.

60. You cannot polish a turd. But you cannot smear precious stones on someone's doorstep as a warning.

61. If the answer's in the question, the question's not big enough.

62. Some pistachios won't open.

63. Outrageousness is a parasite on banality.

64. Fanaticism is blind focus.

65. If eyes are the window to the soul, the mouth is the toilet.

66. Chocolate, especially when melted, reminds us of the thin line between food and diarrhoea.

67. Our convictions don't require courage; we require courage for the exile caused by our convictions.

68. You cannot change the past, but you can alter the data.

69. There are two types of people: those who know they're assholes and assholes.

70. Most would rather lose their life than lose control.

71. No one has a crueller master than the self-employed.

72. Most predictions are puffed-up descriptions.

73. The class system gives landownership the illusion of flair.

74. The only thing keeping us safe is the lottery of decency.

75. The only ugliness is bad taste.

76. The beautiful avert their gaze.

77. Speech is song gone sour.

78. Thoughts search us out, but we are nowhere to be found.

79. People cannot hear you if you speak too loudly.

80. We came from nothing, and that's what we'll come to.

81. What genius starts, some genius finishes.

82. Language is industrial intelligence; television is industrial sabotage.

83. Ripeness is the first stage of decay.

84. Close your eyes and you will see. But maybe pull over first.

85. We all have the need to occupy a reality beyond the one we can apprehend. And also, in an ideal world, off-street parking.

86. 'To be without hope is understandable; to be without despair is inconceivable' is true, but not all children can accept it, especially at night.

87. The inevitable is often preventable.

88. One thing unites us: an overdeveloped interest in ourselves.

Part Two

The Problem with People: Forty-Eight Thoughts Concerning the Folly of Others

1. You call someone 'bright' when the word 'intelligent' isn't appropriate.

2. I now realise the only way to empathise with those who lack empathy is to not even try in the first place.

3. Only the eminent remind us to be humble.

4. The only thing worse than someone who thinks they're always right is a group of people who think they're always right.

5. A lot of people who think they're 'not enough' are, in fact, too much.

6. When I watch people watching sport, I'm reminded of the lengths people will go to avoid talking to one another.

7. Speaking out is often the occupation of the inactive.

8. Why do boring people keep talking to me? Don't they prefer their own kind?

9. I don't think anyone in a hot-air balloon should be calling themselves a pilot.

10. Why does everyone want to look similarly unique?

11. The people who say 'You can't say anything any more' still seem to be saying a lot.

12. People will embrace you for as long as you can further their schemes.

13. People who 'break their silence' are seldom the silent type.

14. When people say that something is so amazing that they 'can't describe it in words', they don't seem to consider that the fault might lie with them, rather than with words.

15. When people say, 'In all honesty . . .', they may be overestimating their capacity for honesty.

16. In conversation, it's frustrating when the other person departs from the script you're imagining.

17. While I accept that others have the right to exist, I want to make it clear that I was not consulted.

18. I can't help but feel that those who can sleep at night just don't get it.

19. A sudden interest in politics seems to correlate more closely to an increase in self-concern than an increase in concern for others.

20. Talk is cheap. Unless you once held public office. In which case, a fee can be arranged.

21. I think there are still one or two people who *aren't* special, and our job is getting them to admit it.

22. Those who are most proud of their country also seem to be the most disgusted by it.

23. People would sooner talk about their problems than solve them.

24. People bemoan passive aggression. Which is totally up to them.

25. The wealthy wear loafers because they like to look casual while stepping over others.

26. When people say they believe in ghosts, it makes me question my belief in people.

27. What's even better than your impression is seeing you trying to moderate your pride while doing your impression.

28. A: Why are you telling me that your dog isn't normally like this?
B: Why are you trying to posit me as a variable in your dog's otherwise blameless existence?
C: Why can't you accept that maybe you and this animal aren't as simpatico as you thought?

29. I split my time between seeing people and recovering from seeing people.

30. When people say something's like a knife through their heart, they're probably not saying that from experience.

31. People who say 'Listen' should focus on making what they say listenable.

32. The very sociable seem unable to extend their sociability to the lonely.

33. When people say 'at the end of the day', don't they mean . . . night?

34. If you say 'snow', some people get cold.

35. No one thanks you for your slow response, even though that's the one that took some thought.

36. It's very important to listen to people, but we must never underestimate the joy of ignoring them.

37. When people talk about how important it is to be in the moment, it doesn't feel like they're really in the moment.

38. We cannot control other people. But we're working on it.

39. Those who say they work to live often seem like hard work.

40. A person is a particular collision of specificities. Your job is to reduce him to one dominant characteristic.

41. You can't take a person's behaviour personally.

42. If paranoia is thinking the world is against you, I don't think we need a specific word for that.

43. It is hard to see past the faults of others, so why not lie back and enjoy the view?

44. The rich walk slowly because they know there's no real way to overtake them.

45. Don't be defensive; others are simply helping us better see our worthlessness.

46. People would rather have freedom of speech than freedom of thought.

47. People who aren't defensive rarely have much to be defensive about. But it's worth attacking them anyway.

48. When someone tells you they've met someone who gives them hope for the future, they tend to be stuck in the past.

Part Three

The Young
(How to Subdue Them);
Friendships
(How to Avoid Them);
Relationships
(How to Win Every
Power Battle);
and Family
(How to Minimise
Its Hold)

1. How come my children have no idea how cool I am?

2. Did it ever occur to you how upsetting it is to me that you're upset with me?

3. It takes a village to raise a child; it takes a city to ignore one.

4. A family is a cult in which the main belief system is itself.

5. My mother used to say, 'Manners maketh the man,' but I didn't think it was very mannerly of her to make fun of my lisp.

6. My dad used to say, 'Wherever you may be, let the wind go free.' But I think it was just an excuse for his relentless guffing.

7. Perhaps the reason so many relationships are toxic is because they have nuclear origins.

8. While renewing their vows, a husband said of his wife, 'She lights up any room she's in.' But is that a good thing? Some of us were trying to sleep.

9. My mother used to say, 'You're nothing without your health.' But I like to think that I'm nothing in my own right.

10. In friendship, one of the hardest things to do is to help the other person understand his or her faults. But now we have the internet.

11. The child is father to the man, but when the child gets ice cream, the man still has to pay.

12. It's hard to say why I have no friends. I mean, who would I say it to?

13. If you're in a romantic mood, and your significant other isn't, maybe try cleaning the toilet, but in a suggestive way. They'll soon get the idea. And if they don't, well, at least you've cleaned the toilet!

14. When you told me I had no feelings, it hurt my feelings, but I didn't let on.

15. Keeping in touch rarely involves touching.

16. People like you telling me I'm completely unreadable is why I don't show my feelings in the first place.

17. Yes, you could call my face expressionless, or you could say my expressions are subtle, non-intrusive and bordering on the indiscernible. But you're too busy gesticulating in wild dismay.

18. It used to be that children imitated their parents. Now children are imitating their parents imitating children.

19. When our friends fail, we grieve, for they will not be able to share our laughter.

20. A home is more than just a house. It is also a place where packages are delivered.

21. If someone is being mean to you, you have a choice: you can try to destroy them . . . and I forget the other option.

22. In arguments, it is important to listen to what the other person is saying. This is called 'gathering evidence'.

23. Friendship isn't just a mutually advantageous, quasi-tribal alliance, used to secure one's societal position and construct a sense of self; it also means having to go to birthday parties.

24. It's hard to say 'sorry', especially with a straight face.

25. 'Sorry' isn't hard to say, it's just hard to mean.

26. Your job is to support your spouse in helping you see how you don't support your spouse.

27. Maybe my way of engaging *is* to withdraw.

28. People need to have their emotions recognised and validated, but often it works just as well if you pretend.

29. Love is more than a word, but we can only say how it's more than a word by using more words, so what's your plan now, Captain Clever?

30. The good thing about envy is that you don't need to have anything in order to enjoy it.

31. A wedding is a funeral for your friends.

32. It's not a disagreement, it's a refusal to participate in your demented reality.

33. Blood is thicker than water, but try washing the car with it.

34. Before he died, I just wanted my father to acknowledge that I didn't need his approval, and that that ought to count for something, but they couldn't resuscitate him in time.

35. I sometimes think of all the things I failed to ask old Ben before he died. But mostly I wish I'd asked him to lend me money.

36. I've made countless mistakes in life, but the real work is shifting culpability onto others.

37. A good place to publicly wash dirty linen is the laundrette.

38. I asked Dad for a fish, but instead of giving me a fish, he said that he would teach me to fish; that way I'd always be able to feed myself. 'When?' I said. 'Now,' he said. 'Where?' I said. 'The sea,' he said. 'But the sea is so far away,' I said. 'Get in the truck,' he said. 'I'll explain the basics as we go.' I was so hungry I found it hard to concentrate, and by the time we were on the water it was getting pretty dark, but he said he wasn't going to let either of us leave the catamaran until we caught something. It was the next morning before we snagged a tiny eel that looked like it had emerged from Satan's own anus. I was delirious with hunger and ready to eat it raw, but Dad said we couldn't: eel blood is poisonous. Then he said I would never amount to anything because I didn't understand people. He wasn't always the best dad, come to think of it.

39. Sometimes I think everyone would be better off without me, but then I remember the will I had my legal team draw up, and I start to laugh.

40. People are very concerned about the effects of mobile phones on children, and I agree. What was wrong with the old-fashioned ways of ignoring the young? I forget what they were now. Maybe we just left them in the car?

41. How can we live without community? The modern world is an attempt to answer that question.

42. I was asked to give a speech at my old school, and I couldn't think of anything to say. I had no words of wisdom, no encouragement to offer. I hadn't learned anything. I was a fraud, a waste of an education. Worse, I was an enemy of education, an illustration of all that was wrong with scholastic achievement at the expense of inner depth. And then I woke up. It was just a stress dream. But how did I manage to fall asleep during my own speech? I blacked out, and the cycle of shame began once more.

43. Candlelit dinners can create a wonderfully intimate ambience, but do you know what's even more romantic? Making sure a fully trained fire officer is present throughout.

44. It is very important to listen, but, in practice, nodding works just as well.

45. If children are our future, what'll we do with them in the meantime?

46. There are no wives of saints, because wives know there are no saints.

47. Don't resort to recriminations. Always strike first.

48. I feel so moved when I hear children practising a musical instrument, because I remember that some things don't get better.

Part Four

Stories We Tell Ourselves:
Myth, Media and the
Vita Creativa

1. The story of the Little Mermaid is a timely reminder of how men can, if given unconditional devotion and service, come to appreciate the charms of a mute beauty.

2. All movies have become an origin story, and yet we still don't know why we're going to see them.

3. There must be a place for good-quality journalism. We just need to find it.

4. A way of curing writer's block is to stop writing. That way it's not a block, it's a choice.

5. Hollywood cinema:
   FEMALE GAZE: I'm yours.
   MALE GAZE: Lucky you.

6. If you are on a creative-writing course, and the teacher says you can't make a character say something just because it's a good line, you know that teacher hasn't been to the theatre recently.

7. I don't want to jinx it, but with AI we might finally have the technology to make a truly great insect-invasion film.

8. A film is just an excuse to stare at people.

9. The nineteenth-century Danish philosopher Kierkegaard said most people decide on an acceptable level of misery and call that happiness, but now we call it 'a limited series event'.

10. I think a great opening to a film would be a shot of a man on a powerful speedboat skimming across a beautiful sea – but he's not happy. Why???

11. In polite society, the norm was to be amusingly self-deprecating, so that conversation might follow by way of mutually affirming contradiction. Negative to positive – and so, a current might flow. This has been fatally undermined by people speaking well of themselves. Thus, we have a choice: the future of civilisation or podcasts.

12. A movie star is someone who begins to be believable only when they're the sole person on camera.

13. What is light entertainment apart from an over-lit record of the smiling determination to remain thin?

14. Hamlet says, 'To be or not to be. That is the question.' And then, like a typical man, goes on to answer the question himself.

15. *Hamlet* is about someone mansplaining themselves to death.

16. Writing is more to do with omission than.

17. It takes great courage to admit you're wrong. It takes greater courage to admit you don't think you're capable of being wrong. And it takes social media to double down on that.

18. Social media perfectly combines voyeurism and exhibitionism.

19. One of the things people forget about the Beatles is how funny their name is.

20. Despite what montages might have us believe, few things are improved with time.

21. If writing is arguing with oneself, how do you know who's won?

22. In art, we show an idealised version of life. And the advantage to this is you can charge for it.

23. Jokes help to release tension; seriousness causes it.

24. In a movie fight scene, the victor will tell a joke – frequently, a pun that relates to their predicament – before killing their adversary, but they rarely wait for the laugh. Perhaps it's this indifference to response, this one-sided notion of connection, that drove them to kill in the first place.

25. Nothing can content a fool, though television comes close.

26. Sometimes I see a photo of a painter's studio and think, 'What's wrong with you? There's paint *everywhere*!'

27. People fear cancellation. I fear subscription.

28. People love calling well-known entertainers who've made a lot of money 'canny', as if it were somehow shrewd of them to become wildly popular and then collect a proportionately insignificant percentage of the proceeds.

29. I prefer the reality of fiction.

30. You can wait for inspiration to strike, or you can just get on with it. But, on the evidence of this sentence, perhaps it's better to wait.

31. On social media, the most saleable commodity is thoughtlessness.

32. Our deeply human need for stories is just another story we tell ourselves.

33. Only in reviews is *anything* 'uproarious'.

34. To be photographed is to permit a permanent record of one's surface, which is why it so suits the shallow.

35. The beauty of live theatre is that, together, we get to communally experience that near-magical sensation of all being bored at once.

36. If all the world's a stage, I'd like to recast.

37. If all the world's a stage, where will we put the audience?

38. Someone once said that the most frightening thing in cinema is a closed door, but the most frightening thing in life is the closed lid of a train toilet.

39. To be famous is to be recognised for being someone else.

40. In fact, we should call famous people the Celebritariat.

41. Acting is reacting. But to what? Acting. And so the terrible cycle continues.

42. Comedy is more to do with rhythm than content, which is why jazz is so funny.

43. Stand-ups are seldom upstanding.

44. Perhaps the lesson of the story of Narcissus is: never trust a mirror you can drink.

45. If the story of Narcissus were a Hollywood film, Narcissus would *almost* drown and then have a series of underwater adventures, before emerging from the pool, older, wiser and more attractive than ever.

46. Every Hollywood film is based on the fiction that attractive people have to overcome obstacles.

47. Hollywood films almost make us believe that the beautiful, in particular, deserve a happy ending.

48. Stories are a way of coping with time, which is why long ones seem so offensive.

49. Shouldn't autofiction write itself?

50. Publicity is the enemy of sincerity.

51. The main Oscar of the night should be for Best Publicity Campaign.

52. The lesson of the knock-knock joke is that if someone knocked only once, we wouldn't even bother to ask, 'Who's there?'

53. The film industry is merely a subset of the far more valuable business of gossip.

54. Often the satisfying feeling you get at the end of a story is just relief that it's ended.

55. Instead of 'HOLLYWOOD', they should call it 'CHEEKBONES'.

56. Style is simply a matter of how.

57. Naturalness is a style – that of being effortlessly boring.

58. In sport, prize money is a cash settlement for all the time you've wasted.

59. I'll tell you what's a contradiction in terms: 'sports personality'.

60. The previously held assumption that some thoughts aren't fit for broadcast is one that podcasting has done much to challenge.

61. If writing is rewriting, why's it wrong to rewrite history?

62. Why do bands choose to make some of their songs less good than their hits?

63. When you see a guitarist leave their cigarette to smoke away under the strings in the headstock, I always expect the guitar to run out of breath halfway through the solo.

64. If you think you can kill a man, but you can't kill an idea, you should watch that man's stand-up special.

65. Fame is the public face of self-deception.

66. Much like a comedian, conscience dies without a good audience.

67. Super-villains, one must admit, at least have a strong sense of their own backstory.

68. Fame is when the public participates in your self-delusion.

69. Anyone can have integrity; it takes talent to sell out.

70. Newspapers print what they think the news ought to be.

71. Cancel culture is scandal solemnised.

72. Boredom is a quarrel with time; music is an attempt to structure it.

Part Five – The Finale

Private Lessons:
Two Hundred and
Twenty-Three Things
I've Taught Myself
the Hard Way

1. If, when one door shuts, another door opens, there's something wrong with your doors. They shouldn't be doing that.

2. TV detectives need a gimmick. Mine would be not caring who did it.

3. If I could live my life again, I'd get better internet.

4. It would be kinder if you stopped telling me to be kind.

5. Self-delusion is what I do best. That and most kinds of science.

6. I wanted to be a glam-rocker, but I'm susceptible to conjunctivitis.

7. I've been diagnosed with a new kind of personality disorder: zero.

8. Every time I go to the toilet I think, 'Really? Again?'

9. My therapist told me that I was avoidant. I said I didn't want to get into it.

10. I don't so much think as brainstorm anxiety.

11. People are so proud about speaking out. But is it possible to speak 'in'?

12. Speaking out is often the occupation of the inactive.

13. If I ever finish writing a book, I want to call it *Incomplete*, because when it gets bad reviews, it will seem like the reviewers formed their judgements too soon.

14. I still can't get over the fact that some people think God is more important than me.

15. I'm a self-hating agnostic: I don't know how best to despise myself.

16. When buying trousers, always get the next size up.

17. Sometimes I think, 'What are we here on this earth to do except to give and receive love?' But then I think, 'What about sanitation? Who's going to deal with that? It better not be me.'

18. When bad fortune comes our way, we can transform it and give it meaning. But I prefer to complain.

19. Someone once said, 'It is never too late to be what you might have been.' Well, I wanted to be a child movie star.

20. People say that success often comes from failure, so where does failure come from?

21. Never, in my whole life, have I met a circle that's even slightly vicious.

22. How do you know when you're old? When people start calling you 'sharp'.

23. Recently, I've started to see warnings about 'historical' attitudes that I might find offensive. But what I find offensive is the implication that it is even possible to have an ahistorical attitude . . .

24. Or: the thing that I find offensive is your prediction of my offence.

25. It's hard work to work this little.

26. 'How can you say nothing?' I didn't say.

27. The first thing I'd do if I were in space would be to stop all the flashing equipment from making those beeping sounds.

28. I don't like being called 'unique'. Why *aren't* more people like me? What's wrong with them?

29. I was on a plane once and saw a fly that had got trapped in the cabin. And I thought, 'This trip is absolutely wasted on you.'

30. To me, the only point of having cake is to eat it too. Who are these cake archivists? And why are they telling me how to live?

31. When arguing with myself, it's hard to know which side to take.

32. I think 'pillow talk' should refer to anything that sounds muffled.

33. Sometimes I look at the world and feel despair, that there is no hope and that existence is an unending interchange of cruelty. But, most of the time, I look away.

34. People often say, 'There isn't a cloud in the sky.' But they fail to mention how cloud-free other places are. I'm thinking of, e.g., shops that sell knick-knacks.

35. 'I don't feel part of any community,' I said, in my opening address at Individualists Anonymous. But the reluctant crowd had already started to disperse.

36. In an age of anxiety, I'm a thought leader.

37. If laughter is the best medicine, why does everyone refuse to let me heal them?

38. I don't know how Descartes got to be so certain he *was* thinking. If 'I think, therefore I am' were true, someone who didn't think would cease to exist. And yet, here I am.

39. Choose guilt over resentment. And choose both over liability.

40. The one thing I won't put up with is stoicism.

41. Sometimes I feel that God is a chef who refuses to eat the meal He cooked.

42. I didn't ask to be born; it was only afterwards that the asking began in earnest.

43. If I'm too tired to sleep, and too tired to wake up, should I really have to listen to what happened in your dream?

44. 'What is this "will to live"? I barely have the will to leave' is probably what I'd say to Schopenhauer if I met him in a dream. I can't be sure. Dreams are weird.

45. Only when we get something does its true worthlessness become apparent.

46. When I called up 'Clive' to say I was lost, he didn't care at all. He just wanted his dog back.

47. I don't want to die, but nor do I want to be alive during my funeral.

48. For as long as ice cream is for sale, I refuse to accept that money can't buy you happiness.

49. Crabs probably don't even have a word for 'sideways'.

50. Once the kite is in the air, what then?

51. If you can be your own worst enemy, I think you can also be your own best friend. Or at least a pretty close friend. Definitely more than an acquaintance. I mean, you don't have to *get on* with yourself.

52. If I were a rapper, and someone dissed me, I'd reply, firmly, in a way that made it clear that my feelings were hurt, 'I would appreciate more respectful and boundaried language in any future raps that you bust.' And then I'd ask whoever was holding the bass to drop it, and drop it almost immediately.

53. If I truly didn't care, I still don't think I'd wave my arms in the air.

54. As far as I'm concerned, Mr DJ, I am under zero obligation to make *any* noise.

55. I think a better name for diarrhoea is 'anus puke', but apparently that's not 'medical' enough.

56. You can't be insulted without your permission. And nor can you be insulated. You can, however, be isolated without your permission, with no one to insulate or insult you.

57. If someone who has betrayed you asks to reconnect, a good thing to do is have it go via whoever runs the prison, rather than 'taking matters into your own hands'.

58. I'll tell you what also happens one step at a time: retreat.

59. I don't know why people think living on your knees is so bad. Try living on your elbows.

60. If I were a singer, I'd start each new song by saying, 'If music is the food of love, love's going hungry.' And then I'd make the sound of a power sander.

61. No kind of cargo should be put in shorts.

62. If someone can do no wrong, they're not anyone.

63. Skin-deep graveyards for misguided notions. Or, as you call them, 'tattoos'.

64. Clapping is basically just hitting yourself. That's how much we dislike the success of others.

65. I think the most surprising thing that could happen in a football match would be if all the players suddenly took up a better hobby.

66. I think the end of racism will come when people dislike each other just for being people.

67. If I were Robin Hood, I'd probably keep some money back for expenses.

68. What's the difference between not remembering something and not knowing something? Hope. Your misplaced hope that the knowledge will somehow drop back into your head. A hope that has no reliable timescale. During which I just have to stand here, waiting.

69. If I were king, and the queen could not produce an heir, and I was in England during the sixteenth century, I'd just be chill, because you can't force these things.

70. Whoever came up with the term 'chillax' probably deemed the words 'chill' and 'relax' both insufficiently descriptive of a truly easeful state of tranquil repose, and that must've started to rankle.

71. While I don't want to dispute the advice to fight fire with fire, isn't that what a fire already is?

72. W/r/t firefighters: does the fire even know it's in a fight?

73. Most kindnesses are judgements in disguise. That's why I refuse to be civil to others. I respect them too much.

74. Can you imagine life before vitamin supplements? It must have been absolutely meaningless.

75. If I had to be in the police, I think I would choose to serve in the grammar department.

76. If you do want to be king of the castle, you can't wait for someone else to appoint you. You have to seize sovereignty.

77. If someone asks you a direct question, you should feel free to ask them a question back. Like, 'What do *you* think I'm doing with your wallet?'

78. I bet if my torso were photographed and put on a billboard, no one would even know it was mine.

79. I think anyone who says that the guitar is a phallic object has an overly optimistic idea of what penises can achieve.

80. If, after passing a stool, the bowl is filled with black, semi-congealed blood, just think, 'That's probably normal for a vampire.'

81. If I were preparing for a vampire attack and I'd ordered garlic online, and the delivery person said that there'd been a substitution and they were offering shallots instead, I feel that would put me in a very difficult position.

82. I've seen stained-glass windows. I don't think those stains are coming out.

83. If you have an idea, you've got to write it down right away because it won't be good enough to remember.

84. The thing I find most disgusting about rats is how intent they are on survival.

85. Much of my malice is an afterthought.

86. When I look back at myself in the past, I think, 'Who is that person? And how can he be stopped?' And then I think, 'Who's stopping me now? Me in the future, I guess.'

87. I often wonder why we sleep, but during the sleep itself, it seems to make sense.

88. I'm very open about how hidden I am.

89. I'm not self-obsessed. I'm steadfast in my self-interest.

90. I'm not funny. I'm a serious person whom no one takes seriously.

91. If I were being executed, my last meal would be something light. There's something depressing about dying *and* feeling too full. Like, 'What's wrong with me? I'm *out of control.*'

92. People say dogs are man's best friend, but given that dogs rely on man for food, water, access to mates and, in many cases, touch, I'd say that dogs are trapped in a man cult.

93. The soundtrack of my life is me talking.

94. People mistake me for being intelligent because I don't seem to have any other qualities. But that is a mistake. I am not intelligent either.

95. I think clouds enjoy their own company.

96. It takes great courage to admit you're wrong; it takes greater courage to randomly accuse someone else.

97. They say fools rush in, but I've seen a lot of them just slowly milling about.

98. If you do bring a knife to a gunfight, suggest a 'no shooting' policy.

99. People say insects have no soul, and that seems fair enough. Though I think caterpillars have a sadness to them.

100. I don't know that there is a school of thought. If there is, attendance is poor.

101. Just saw a bunch of fish. They weren't studying.

102. If I stopped apologising, I could carve out more time to do things which require an apology.

103. If two wrongs don't make a right, how many *does* it take?

104. *You* go to gate.

105. Conversation is an art, and I don't believe in art for art's sake.

106. I don't think I should call it 'breakfast'. The only reason I stopped eating was because I had to go to sleep.

107. Being early is a waste of my time.

108. If dogs have such good hearing, how come more of them don't pursue music?

109. Do security guards ever wonder why they have the only job that can also be done by a dog?

110. When sniffer dogs detect a bomb, what does it smell like to them? Probably sausages.

111. One of the least punk things is when a streaming service recommends you punk.

112. I think it's more punk to swallow your phlegm.

113. I don't think I'll ever retire. I'll just carry on doing nothing.

114. I told her: when two men are trying to help a woman understand something, the correct term is 'mensplaining'.

115. Pirates' short-term plans seem clear. But what of the long term?

116. I bet there are plenty of pirates who start to question the morality of pillaging but can't give up the lifestyle.

117. In terms of engendering fear, I don't really know what the crossbones add to the image of a skull.

118. Q: Without health, what am I?
    A: Me.

119. I'm not afraid of dying, as long as it doesn't kill me.

120. Yes, it's important to acknowledge your feelings, but what about my feeling of boredom?

121. But did anyone aspire to be the manufacturer of aspirational bumper stickers?

122. We speak in order to convince ourselves we have something to say.

123. Those who tend to their gardens tend to go on about it.

124. Edgy people tend not to use the word 'edgy'.

125. Re mic drops: dynamic microphones are rarely damaged by impact. It would be more 'rock 'n' roll' to corrode your mic – e.g. by leaving it in water for a prolonged period.

126. Aren't rhetorical questions more like statements?

127. If, as human beings, we're wired for connection, I'm on a closed circuit.

128. If all the animals could just get organised, I think they could beat us once and for all.

129. If you gave a mosquito a whole bag of blood, I bet it wouldn't even say thank you.

130. Nowadays, the word 'crazy' carries an understandable stigma. But how else can we describe the sheer scale of these discounts?

131. Has pain been killed yet?

132. It's hard to stop yourself from falling into bitterness. My advice is just to relax and slide right into it.

133. Nothing's impossible, apart from, therefore, finding any use for the word 'impossible'.

134. If I wrote an autobiography, I'd call it *I Shouldn't Make It Up*.

135. If I went by just one name, like an indifferent pop star or Hercules, and I were also a spy, and someone was about to blow my cover, I'd say, 'Shh! I'm trying to remain mononymous.' And then hope that they didn't laugh so loud that they blew my cover.

136. What if today isn't a new day?

137. If today is the first day of the rest of my life, what the hell was yesterday? Because if it was the last day of my former life, that's a shame.

138. If I receive flowers, I just think, 'Great – here's another formerly living thing that's been cut off from everything that nourishes it.'

139. To strengthen the mind, one must exercise it. The only solution I've come up with is shaking my head very fast.

140. I'm not sure I want the kind of truth that's already been handled.

141. 'I decide what's true' is a good sentence to slip into a job interview, just to make sure that they really want you.

142. 'To live is to submit to the lie that living is worth it' is a hard sentence to come back from, socially, especially at a prize-giving.

143. Maybe pots should try to see beyond race.

144. Thinking alike is not direct evidence of greatness.

145. A bad workman blames his tools – which is a pretty rude way to describe his fellow workmen.

146. Pleasure *is* my business.

147. Are you insinuating that the fixity of a leopard's spots is a design flaw?

148. Must we answer silly questions seriously?

149. I've tried being myself. It didn't feel like me.

150. Some say clothes don't make the man. Some say clothes maketh the man. I say, 'For God's sake, put a top on.'

151. Are comparisons really odious, or are you just threatened by my commitment to match any price?

152. I am counting my blessings; it's just not taking very long.

153. The cream rises to the top only in very specific circumstances.

154. If I choose to surrender, does that mean I'm still in charge?

155. I bet the problem with being an arsonist is what to do for the summer holidays, because you're probably sick to death of heat.

156. Maybe the book is letting the cover down.

157. That pen's not your pal.

158. The making *is* the faking.

159. Not only does everyone have their price, but often there's a group discount.

160. If you were truly present, wouldn't you be too present to know what it was to be present? And would you take time out of your being so massively present to tell me how important it was?

161. If I saw a popular band disembarking from a yacht or a cruiser, I hope I'd have the presence of mind to say, 'I hope you didn't rock the boat,' but I'd probably just keep walking.

162. If you manage to make a mountain out of a molehill, I think you deserve praise, because look what you started with!

163. Maybe the real problem is that apple carts can't emotionally regulate.

164. I think what's even funnier than saying 'Touch wood' and touching your head would be if you then buffed your head with a power sander while the air filled with sawdust.

165. Regardless of your ethical stance, I think it's a stretch to call an unhatched chicken a chicken, at least for advertising purposes.

166. When someone says, 'Define your terms,' a good thing to say is, 'Define "define",' and then disappear in a puff of pink smoke.

167. 'If you want something done well, do it yourself,' I said. But, secretly, I was worried whether my lack of surgical experience would tell. But, by that point, the anaesthetic had started to kick in and I'd already shaved my head.

168. They say, 'Teach a man to fish,' but is it a degree?

169. If I were an alchemist, I'd try to turn diarrhoea into gold, because then I think I'd be less resentful about having constant diarrhoea.

170. What's strange is that if you look up the definition of 'mathematics' in the dictionary, it doesn't even mention how boring it is.

171. The difference between skiing and skidding has yet to become clear.

172. They say aim for the moon, but with what?

173. Why aren't there more twenty-four-hour stationery shops?

174. If I had been a Mongol emperor, my first target would have been to cut pillaging by 10 per cent.

175. When I called you an 'icon', I meant you were a two-dimensional relic lacking perspective.

176. They say when you find yourself in darkness, instead of complaining, light a candle. But what if you were trying to tell people you could smell gas?

177. The way to a man's heart is through his stomach, but what's the way out? I bet the pipes in there are smaller than you think. Maybe through the neck?

178. If you were selling a car to a gangster, I think the way to clinch the deal would be to emphasise the generous boot space.

179. Why isn't everyone else panicking on my behalf?

180. If inspiration is 90 per cent perspiration, maybe I'm some kind of deodorant?

181. When strangers, often in the street, shout out, 'I love you!' I tell them I'm sorry they're in such a toxic, non-reciprocal relationship. But not out loud. I look down at the pavement and, as calmly as I can, flick the safety off my taser.

182. I'm not punching down; I'm lending a hand.

183. I'm not punching down; I'm just out of reach.

184. Nobody. That's what I call my head.

185. I feel people's prime source of dopamine has become saying the word 'dopamine'.

186. Justifying the work I'm not doing is a full-time job.

187. When you eat a Conference pear, that's the end of the meeting.

188. Progressivism is pessimism about the past; conservatism is pessimism about the future; but few things are less progressive than rock.

189. Simply put, racism places unnecessary parameters on one's misanthropy. Why limit your hatred?

190. Is there any knowledge which is so certain that no reasonable man might doubt it? And, if not, why am I paying so much for my car insurance?

191. They say life is what you make of it. So, is death what you don't make of it?

192. When did the word 'enjoy' start to be used, almost solely, as a command?

193. To be free is to be too short-sighted to see the walls. To be imprisoned is to believe that the walls are real. But don't try to walk through those walls. Because they are real, and you're in jail, and you know why.

194. You cannot be cancelled unless you accept the commission.

195. To be self-employed is to make everyone else your boss.

196. To demean a tree is to mock on wood.

197. The people who say you should not mock others often look like they have skin in the game.

198. They say an army marches on its stomach, but isn't that just crawling?

199. If provoked, I can be tender.

200. I hope to be remembered more for what I didn't do.

201. Never gift a horse to an equine dentist. I mean, what are they meant to do? *Not* look at it in the mouth?

202. Is a moral vacuum too good to clean a carpet, or not good enough?

203. When you dream that you are dreaming, you *are* close to waking, but the important thing is to please not tell me about it.

204. No one is naturally tidy; the factory setting is laziness.

205. Only by wearing a mask can I be myself, which, I suppose, is someone who likes to rob banks.

206. I'll tell you what really is 'all form and no content': a form.

207. A mistake is merely a preview of what you'll do next time.

208. I only pretend to be myself.

209. They say sarcasm is a last resort, but I think it's a fun place to visit any time.

210. Have fun. Just don't do it in front of me.

211. In politics, God's the enemy. In show business, God's the competition.

212. Comedians permit us to delight in our own good humour.

213. It's amazing to think that much of Shakespeare's love poetry pre-dated deodorant.

214. A reformed Lothario simply knows the jig is up; or rather, not up enough.

215. Progress is repetitive.

216. A funfair is neither.

217. Social media is proof that there's a despair even greater than data management.

218. If I were a barber, the first thing I'd say to a client would be, 'Sure, we can cut it, but it'll probably grow right back.'

219. Human evolution has tipped. What we have now are small minds in big heads.

220. For those in show business, an obituary is one more review.

221. If you can call it a 'selfie', you're probably the kind of person who should take one.

222. If the Hippocratic oath asks doctors to do no harm, who in hell is performing all these bum lifts?

223. After bantz comes silentz.